THEMATIC UNIT
NATIVE AMERICANS

Written by Leigh Hoven

Illustrated by Blanqui Apodaca and Paula Spence

Teacher Created Materials, Inc.
6421 Industry Way
Westminster, CA 92683
www.teachercreated.com

©1990 Teacher Created Materials, Inc.

Reprinted, 2002

Made in U.S.A.

ISBN-1-55734-285-7

Table of Contents

INTRODUCTION

Native Americans contains a captivating whole language, thematic unit. Its 80 exciting pages are filled with a wide variety of lesson ideas and reproducible pages designed for use with intermediate children. At its core are three high-quality children's literature selections, *Annie and the Old One, The Gift of the Sacred Dog,* and a poetry book, *The Desert Is Theirs.* For each of these books activities are included which set the stage for reading, encourage the enjoyment of the book, and extend the concepts gained. In addition, the theme is connected to the curriculum with activities in language arts (including daily writing suggestions), math, science, social studies, art, music, and life skills (cooking, physical education, career awareness, etc.) Many of these activities encourage cooperative learning. Suggestions and patterns for bulletin boards and unit management tools are additional time savers for the busy teacher. Futhermore, directions for student-created Big Books and a culminating activity, which allow students to synthesize their knowledge in order to produce products that can be shared beyond the classroom, highlight this very complete teacher resource.

This thematic unit includes:

❏ **literature selections**—summaries of three children's books with related lessons (complete with reproducible pages) that cross the curriculum

❏ **poetry**—suggested selections and lessons enabling students to write and publish their own works

❏ **planning guides**—suggestions for sequencing lessons each day of the unit

❏ **writing ideas**—daily suggestions as well as writing activities across the curriculum, including Big Books

❏ **bulletin board ideas**—suggestions and plans for student-created and/or interactive bulletin boards

❏ **homework suggestions**—extending the unit to the child's home

❏ **curriculum connections**—in language arts, math, science, social studies, art, music, and life skills such as cooking, physical education, and career awareness group projects—to foster cooperative learning

❏ **a culminating activity**—which requires students to synthesize their learning to produce a product or engage in an activity that can be shared with others

❏ **a bibliography**—suggesting additional literature and non-fiction books on the theme

---

To keep this valuable resource intact so that it can be used year after year, you may wish to punch holes in the pages and store them in a three-ring binder.

INTRODUCTION *(cont.)*

WHY WHOLE LANGUAGE?

A whole language approach involves children in using all modes of communication: reading, writing, listening, observing, illustrating, experiencing, and doing. Communication skills are interconnected and integrated into lessons that emphasize the whole of language rather than isolating its parts. The lessons revolve around selected literature. Reading is not taught as a separate subject from writing and spelling, for example. A child reads, writes (spelling appropriately for his/her level), speaks, listens, etc. in response to a literature experience introduced by the teacher. In this way, language skills grow naturally, stimulated by involvement and interest in the topic at hand.

WHY THEMATIC PLANNING?

One very useful tool for implementing an integrated whole language program is thematic planning. By choosing a theme with correlating literature selections for a unit of study, a teacher can plan activities throughout the day that lead to a cohesive, in-depth study of the topic. Students will be practicing and applying their skills in meaningful contexts. Consequently, they will tend to learn and retain more. Both teachers and students will be freed from a day that is broken into unrelated segments of isolated drill and practice.

WHY COOPERATIVE LEARNING?

Besides academic skills and content, students need to learn social skills. No longer can this area of development be taken for granted. Students must learn to work cooperatively in groups in order to function well in modern society. Group activities should be a regular part of school life and teachers should consciously include social objectives as well as academic objectives in their planning. For example, a group working together to write a report may need to select a leader. The teacher should make clear to the students and monitor the qualities of good leader-follower group interaction just as he/she would state and monitor the academic goals of the project.

WHY BIG BOOKS?

An excellent cooperative, whole language activity is the production of Big Books. Groups of students, or the whole class, can apply their language skills, content knowledge, and creativity to produce a Big Book that can become a part of the classroom library to be read and reread. These books make excellent culminating projects for sharing beyond the classroom with parents, librarians, other classes, etc. Big Books can be produced in many ways and this thematic unit book includes directions for at least one method you may choose.

Annie and the Old One

by Miska Miles

Annie's Navejo world was good until the Old One (her grandmother) announced to the family that when the rug being woven was finished, she would... "go to Mother Earth." As the story unfolds we learn not only about Annie and her family but also about the contemporary Navejo people—their strength, their life style and their beliefs. This book deals with a very sensitive subject in a beautiful and caring way. Children can easily relate to Annie as she tries to prevent her mother and grandmother from finishing the rug.

The outline below is a suggested plan for using the various activities that are presented in this unit. You should adapt these ideas to fit your own classroom situation.

Sample Plan

Day I

- Daily Writing Activities (see pages 38-40)
- Research the Navajo (use page 8 and other sources)
- Study desert geography—Use bulletin board (pages 76-78)
- Make Tissue Paper Desert art project (page 9)
- Begin homework—"Me" Collage (page 10)

Day II

- Continue Daily Writing Activities (pages 38-40)
- Learn about hogans (page 11)
- Build a hogan (page 12)
- Learn Hogan Chant (page 59)
- Read pages 3-6 from *Annie and the Old One*
- Homework: Finish "Me" Collage (page 10)

Day III

- Continue Daily Writing Activities (pages 38-40)
- Share "Me" Collages
- Read pages 6-16 from *Annie and the Old One*
- Write Reading Response Journals (see pages 13-15)
- Complete tissue paper scene by adding hogan, corral, sheep and loom
- Introduce Weaving (page 16)

Day IV

- Continue Daily Writing Activities (pages 38-40)
- Read pages 19-36 from *Annie and the Old One*
- Work on Reading Response Journals
- Make an Annie Collage
- Character Web—Annie (pages 41-42)
- Start a diary for Annie or the Old One
- Continue weaving

Day V

- Finish reading *Annie and the Old One*
- Work on Reading Response Journals
- Story Pyramid, Annie (pages 41 and 43)
- Make Big Book (may take more than one day); see page 7
- Make and eat Fry Bread (page 63)
- Finish weaving

Overview of Activities

Setting the Stage

1. Introduce Attendance Graphing/Daily Writing Activities. Complete directions and suggestions are on pages 38 to 40.

2. Make the Desert Bulletin Board (see pages 76-78). Begin with the physical features and add the animals, plants, and homes as they are mentioned in the books, *Annie and the Old One* and *The Desert Is Theirs*. Be sure that the students understand the vocabulary words "mesa" and "bluff."

3. Have the students make their own individual tissue paper desert scene (see page 9). This can become the cover for their Reading Response Journal or Annie's Diary (both are described later in this section).

4. Introduce the "Me" Collage (page 10). Tell the students that a collage is an art form that uses overlapping pictures to convey information and/or express an idea. Have magazines available to begin the activity in class. You may need to allow more than one day for this. When the activity is completed, allow time for the students to share orally and to write about their collages.

5. Give the students background information on the Navajo. Reproduce page 8. Obtain as many books on the Navajo as possible. See Bibliography, page 79, for suggested titles. Read information with the total group. Use the world and United States maps to supplement the information.

6. Read and discuss About the Hogan (page 11). Show photos and/or pictures if available. Role-play the males and females entering the hogan.

7. In cooperative groups, have the students create a Navajo diorama. Use the hogan pattern (page 12). Put the hogans on a piece of cardboard. Add sand, a loom, a corral, sheep and other details to create the surrounding area.

8. Learn the Hogan Chant on page 59. Have the cooperative groups practice the chant with instruments. (Directions for making many instruments are on page 55 to 58.) Create another verse. Perform chant for the class.

Enjoying the Book

1. Read aloud the beginning of the book (pages 3-6, stopping after the first paragraph on page 6). Discuss the setting, noting whether students are able to use the vocabulary introduced in Setting the Stage.

2. Introduce the Reading Response Journal. Teacher directions are on page 13. Students complete pages 14 and 15. Model how to respond. Allow them time to write (without worrying about form or correctness) and to share. It is important for the teacher to write a comment in each child's journal as often as possible. They need to know that their thoughts and ideas are respected and important. Accept all reasonable comments. This takes teacher time, but the greater depth of the student responses will be worth it. Research tells us that a personal response to literature is critical to a student becoming a life-long reader.

Overview of Activities *(cont.)*

3. Read pages 6-16 from *Annie and the Old One* (use either as a teacher read-aloud or use for student reading if enough copies are available). As the students read, have them do reading response journal entries (see page 13) and allow time for them to share their thoughts with each other and with you.

4. Have the students add a loom, hogan, corral and sheep to their tissue paper desert scenes. Use construction paper, crayon, or a combination.

5. Introduce the weaving activity. (Complete directions are on pages 16 and 17.) Allow students to work on the weaving for a short time each day during the reading of the book. This should not be completed in one session. It can become tedious! Done a little at a time, as Navajo blankets were done, it complements the story.

6. Read pages 19-36 from *Annie and the Old One*, following the procedure described in number 3 above.

7. Have students make a collage from Annie's point of view. They can compare it to theirs both orally and in writing.

8. Have students work with a partner to make a character web of Annie. Teacher directions are on page 41. Students use page 42. To get the students started, model the procedure and then have them finish with their partner.

9. You may wish to have students write a day by day diary from Annie's point of view or from the Old One's point of view.

10. Finish reading *Annie and the Old One*.

11. Create a Story Pyramid for the book (pages 41 and 43).

Extending the Book

1. Make Fry Bread. See directions on page 63. During math, students could double the recipe, etc., whatever is appropriate to their skill level.

2. Make a Big Book. Divide the students into cooperative groups. Three to five students usually make a workable group. Assign each group a page to write and illustrate.

   page 1—The setting

   page 2—The problem, the Old One reveals she is going to die.

   Annie attempts to cope:

   page 3—Trouble at school

   page 4—Annie undoes weaving

   page 5—Annie lets sheep out of corral

   page 6—The solution—Annie accepts and learns to weave

Have each group make the background using the tissue paper technique learned in the tissue paper desert project (page 9) and add details with construction paper or crayon. Beneath each picture the group should write a summary of that part of the book. Assemble the pages into a Big Book.

Name _____

About the Navajo

The Navajo is the largest Native American tribe living in America today. There are about 140,000 and most live on the Navajo Reservation. The reservation is located in the northeast corner of Arizona, a small part of Utah, and a part of New Mexico.

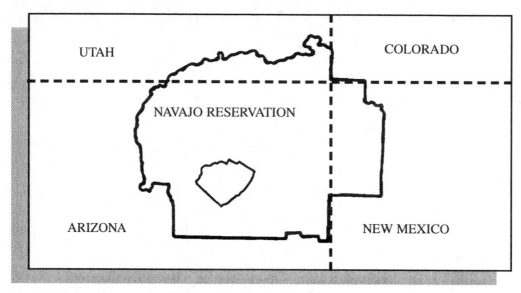

To the Navajo their land is sacred. It includes four sacred mountains—a white mountain, a turquoise blue mountain, a yellow mountain, and a mountain of jet black. The land is a mixture of desert, tall mountains, and deep canyons.

It is believed that the original Navajo people came to North America across the Bering Strait more than 20,000 years ago. These ancestors then migrated from what is now Alaska and Canada to the southwestern United States. They are closely related to the Apache. They settled near the Pueblos who taught them to farm. Early Spanish explorers called them "Apache de Nabaju"—the Apache of the Cultivated Fields. The Navajo call themselves Dine (Din-ay) which means The People.

The Navajo are a bright and adaptable people. They raise sheep which they learned from the Spanish. The art of weaving was learned from the Pueblo. A Navajo rug is a work of art and can sell for several thousand dollars. Silversmithing was learned from Mexican craftsmen. Navajo jewelry is now famous throughout the United States and Mexico.

Use complete sentences to answer the following questions.

1. What states touch the Navajo reservation? _____

   _____

2. How do the Navajo feel about their land? _____

   _____

3. Where did the Navajo come from originally? _____

   _____

4. For what two crafts are the Navajo known? _____

   _____

Tissue Paper Desert

Objective:

To create a desert scene to bring meaning to *Annie and the Old One*.

"Annie's Navajo world was good—a world of rippling sand, of high copper-red bluffs in the distance, of the low mesa near her own snug hogan."

Materials:

9" x 12" white drawing paper—tissue paper: light brown (sand), red and orange (bluffs), brown (mesa), light blue and yellow (sky)—starch—paint brush—shellac (optional)

Directions:

1. Cover workspace with newspaper.

2. Tear uneven strips of light blue tissue paper for the sky.

3. Paint top ⅓ of white paper very lightly with starch. Beginning at the top, lay a blue tissue strip on paper. Gently go over it with starch using paint brush.

4. Continue overlapping light blue tissue in this way until you are about ½ way down the paper.

5. Add a few pieces of yellow tissue in sky for rays of sunlight.

6. Start at the bottom and do the same thing with light brown strips to make the "rippling sand." Don't worry if tissue wrinkles.

7. Cut a mesa from brown tissue. Add to landscape using starch.

8. Cut bluffs from orange and red tissue. Add to landscape.

9. Let dry. Add a few plants with crayon.

10. Shellac if desired.

To Create a CLASS MURAL

Follow the same procedure using butcher paper and glue instead of starch. Add plants, hogan, corral, sheep and a loom. Put weavings done by students together on the loom to form a "class rug."

Name_____

"Me" Collage

Day 1: Collect or draw pictures about yourself below.

Day 2: Cut out the pictures. Add additional pictures and/or words that describe you. Arrange all in an interesting and appeaiing collage. Mount on construction paper.

Me	**My Home**
How I Get to School	**A Chore I Do**
My Family	**Something I'm Learning to Do**
A Time When I Did Something I Shouldn't Have Done	**Animals I Have**

Name_____

About the Hogan

The Navajo home is called a hogan. The early hogan was simply a hole dug out of the ground and covered with a mat of leaves and twigs. As the Navajo became farmers and sheep herders, their homes became more permanent. A present-day hogan sits on top of the ground. It has six sides and a low rounded roof. It is made of logs and adobe mud. The logs are fitted tightly together to form the sides. Then the spaces are packed with mud or clay. There is a single doorway which is covered with a rug. The doorway always faces the first light of day-the east. A hole is made in the roof to let the smoke out.

A hogan is always only one room. Some are large and have tables, chairs, beds, a wood-burning stove and sometimes windows. Outside the hogan there is the loom for weaving. This is brought inside during the winter months. Close by is usually a corral for the herd of sheep.

The Navajo people do not live in villages or even groups of hogans. Their reservation is very large and their homes are far apart. However, when a daughter marries, she and her husband will usually build their new hogan near her mother's.

When a woman enters a hogan, it is the custom for her to go to the right, or north. When a man enters a hogan, he turns left, or south.

After a hogan is built, it is blessed by a special ceremony to bring it good luck and happiness.

Hogan Patterns

Doorway side

Trace and cut 1.

Use brown construction paper or tagboard.

Decorate to look like logs.

Fold and tape

Stovepipe

Trace and cut from black paper.

Roll into a tall tube and glue.

Insert into hole in roof.

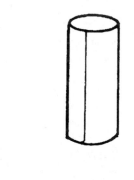

Sides

Trace and cut 5.

Use brown construction paper or tagboard.

Decorate to look like logs.

Fold and tape

1. Join the five sides and doorway piece with tape on the inside to form a hexagon.

2. Glue Tab A of rug to top inside of doorway.

3. Cut an 8" (20 cm) diameter paper circle for roof. (Or use flattened coffee filter or small paper plate.) Cut small hole in center of roof. Attach roof to walls with tape on inside. Insert stovepipe.

4. Set on cardboard base. Add corral, sheep, loom and surroundings to create a Navajo scene.

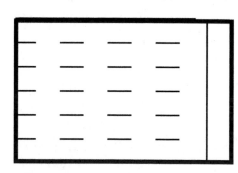

Rug for Doorway

a. Trace and cut from any color.

b. Cut along dashed lines to make a "loom."

c. Weave with strips (about 1 cm x 4 cm) of colored construction paper.

d. Glue at bottom to hold strips in place.

Reading Response Journals

A reading response journal provides students an opportunity to experience the beauty of the author's use of language, to reflect upon the meaning of the text, as well as to personalize the literature. A sample journal for *Annie and the Old One* is on pages 14 and 15. Guide the students to complete these pages. Then, use the directions below to show them how to do their own.

Quote from Text	Student Response

First, have the children draw a line down the middle of the page. Title the left hand side " Quote From Text." Title the right hand side "Student Response." (Stenographers' pads work very well for this). On the left the student copies exactly the words of the author. This gives them another repetition of the language. Since the authors usually use more advanced language and sentence construction than the average student, this is an important step toward improving students' written work. On the right side the student writes his/her response. What do those words mean to him/her? Has he/she ever felt that way? Has he/she ever had that experience? This needs a lot of teacher modeling. Accept ALL student responses. This is NOT to be graded or corrected!

Some students will write a lot on a particular quote and others very little. Much of this depends upon their past experiences. However, having a child take meaning from a piece of literature and relate it to their own life is a critical step in creating the love of literature which is the foundation for creating a life-long reader!

Selected Quotes

Here are selected quotes from the book which you may wish to use. However, you and your students may want to choose others.

"Annie's thoughts wandered. She thought about the stories her grandmother had told-stories of hardships.... "

"'My children, when the new rug is taken from the loom, I will go to Mother Earth.' Annie shivered and looked at her mother. Her mother's eyes were shining bright with tears that did not fall, and Annie knew what her grandmother meant. Her heart stood still and she made no sound."

"When school was over for the day, Annie waited. Timidly, with hammering heart, she went to the teacher's desk. 'Do you want my mother and father to come to school tomorrow?' she asked."

"In school that day, Annie sat quietly and wondered what more she could do. When the teacher asked questions, Annie looked at the floor. She did not even hear."

"Annie wanted to throw her arms around her grandmother's waist and tell her why she had been bad, but she could only stumble to her blanket and huddle under it and let the tears roll into the edge of her hair."

"'My granddaughter,' she said, 'you have tried to hold back time. This cannot be done.'"

Name_____

Reading Response Journal

Read each quote from *Annie and the Old One*. Then write a response from your own experience.

Quote from the book	Response from your own experience
"Annie's Navajo world was good—a world of rippling sand, of high copper-red bluffs in the distance, of the low mesa near her own snug hogan."	_____'s world was good-a world of _____ _____ _____ _____ _____
"Each morning the gate to the night pen near the hogan was opened wide and the sheep were herded to pasture in the desert."	Each morning _____ _____ _____ _____ _____ _____

Name_____

Reading Response Journal *(cont.)*

"Annie helped watch the sheep. She carried pails of water to the cornfield."

_____ helped _____

_____

_____

_____

_____

_____

_____

_____

"And every weekday, she walked to the bus stop and waited for the yellow bus that took her to school and brought her home again."

And every weekday _____

_____

_____

_____

_____

_____

_____

"Best of all were the evenings when she sat at her grandmother's feet and listened to stories of times long gone."

Best of all _____

_____

_____

_____

_____

_____

_____

Weaving

Background

The Navajo adapted and improved the weaving techniques they learned from the Pueblo in the early 1600's. Today they use an upright loom. This skill is mainly practiced by women. Wool for weaving is plentiful since the Navajo are sheep herders.

Relationship to *Annie and the Old One*

In this book the Old One is Annie's grandmother. She knows the skill of weaving. The fact that a rug is being woven is essential to the plot.

Vocabulary

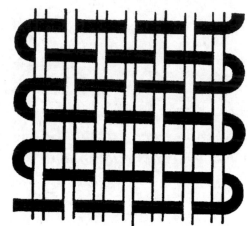

loom   the structure on which one weaves

warp   the vertical threads (strings) which make up the "skeleton" across which the threads are woven

weft   the horizontal threads woven across the warp to form cloth

weave pattern of threads; plain or tabby is the most common, consisting of over one-under one

Weaving on a Box Loom

Materials

1. Shoe box lid or other sturdy, shallow cardboard box
2. Scissors
3. Pencil and ruler
4. Warp string (cotton works best, yarn will stretch)
5. Weft yarn or roving

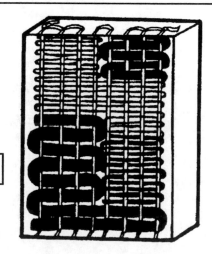

Procedure

Do in 20-30 minute time blocks throughout the unit.

1. Make the loom. With pencil and ruler, make an equal and even number of dots along two opposite edges of box lid.

Weaving *(cont.)*

Procedure *(cont.)*

2. To hold the warp string make notches at the dots. Be sure you have an even number on each side.

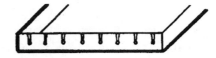

3. Attach the warp string to the box with a knot around the first notch.

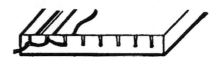

4. Pull the warp across the loom to the opposite notch. Loop around the tab and through the second notch.

5. Pull warp back and forth across the loom until complete. Tie off warp string with a knot.

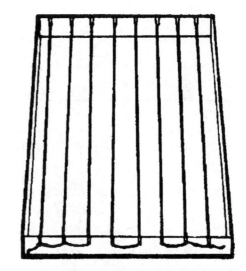

6. The weft: Use a variety of yarns and materials to weave. When you go back and forth, be sure not to pull too tight at the edges. If you do, you will get an hourglass effect. However' it is very important that each line fits tightly to the one above.

7. When you change yarns, leave about 2 inches (5 cm) at the side so you can weave these in later after you have taken the weaving off the loom.

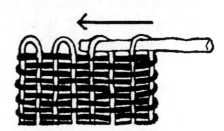

8. When loom is full, remove the weaving. Bend down the tabs and slip carefully off. Slide sticks or twigs through the loops at each end.

Hint: Be sure weaving is tight before removing.

9. Weave loose ends into the back of weaving. Do not cut them off! Weaving will unravel.

10. Display finished product!

The Desert Is Theirs

by Byrd Baylor

Summary

As you read the blend of folklore and fact in the poetic text of this book about the Southwestern U.S. desert, you will also learn about the Papagos. These people know and understand the desert, its plants and animals. They are at home there and live in harmony with nature. Students will have a greater understanding of the desert and the Native American after experiencing this beautiful book and the following activities.

Overview of Activities

Setting the Stage

1. Read and discuss the background information on the Papagos and their legends (page 19).

2. Introduce the book to the students. Explain that the desert area the Papagos inhabit is similar to the area of the Navajo.

Enjoying the Book

1. Read and discuss each page of the book with the children. Be sure to have children note the form of the poetry.

2. As you read the book, have students use the pictures on pages 51 and 52 to make the plants and animals mentioned in *The Desert Is Theirs* in various sizes. Add them to the desert bulletin board with the largest pictures toward the bottom and the smallest at the top to create a feeling of depth and vastness.

3. Create parallel poems. (Page 20 may be used after the first two pages of the book. The second parallel poem, page 21, is based on the text page in the middle of the book where petroglyphs are being drawn on a rock.) Have the students use the left side of the paper to fill in Byrd Baylor's actual words. Model and brainstorm some ideas for the student side.

4. Use Designing Petroglyphs (page 54). This could be done so that it can be added to your bulletin board.

Extending the Book

1. Help students compare their families to the Papago using the Venn diagram on page 22. Model where to put the items that are the same and different; e.g., "like the land they live on," would go in the overlapping section if both families like the area where they live and "live in the desert" would go in the Papago circle if the student's family does not live in the desert. Students should add additional items.

2. For science, make the Desert Guidebook (pages 48-53).

3. Byrd Baylor writes, "Even then Coyote was around giving advice..." For a creative writing activity, have the students draw a coyote at the bottom of a paper, then add a large cartoon type bubble in which to write the coyote's advice.

Name_____

The Papago

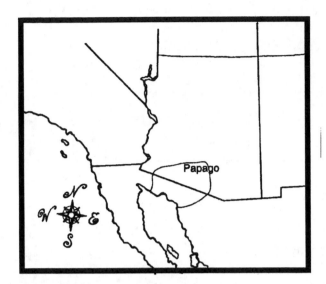

The name of the tribe comes from the word papah, meaning "beans." Their original home was near the Gila River, south of Tucson, Arizona, and went across the desert to Sonora, Mexico. They were a peaceful, farming people who raised maize, beans and cotton. Another source of food was desert plants. They ate the fruit from the giant cactus and from it made a drink for the annual rain ceremony. Their homes were round, with twigs, grass and leafy shrubs on the roof.

The Papago women were excellent basket makers. Their baskets served a double purpose. They were used for cooking, carrying and storing. When dancing and singing began, they were turned over and used as drums. Some were so large that three men could play them at one time by kneeling and striking them with their hands.

Legends

The Papago watched the stars. When they saw Pleiades rise in the east in the evening and set in the west just before sunrise, the time for storytelling began. (The nights when these stars are seen are the longest nights of the year.) They told stories beginning with the creation of the world. Four nights were needed to tell the tribal stories. One of the stories tells of Elder Brother and is similar to Noah's Ark. This legend is woven into the book *The Desert Is Theirs*.

Parallel Poetry

Read and discuss *The Desert Is Theirs*. Use the form of the poetry in that book to write your own poem. In the left column below, copy the indicated sections with the words arranged just as they are in the book. In the right column, add your own words to make an original parallel poem. Use other parts of the book to write your own parallel poems.

Book Text *The Desert Is Theirs*	Student Poem "The Earth Is Ours"
"This is no place	This is no place
_____	for anyone
_____	who wants
_____	bombs
_____	and wars
_____	and everything
_____	red
green…	red
	red…
This is for hawks	This is for people
_____	that like only
_____	
_____	_____
_____	and _____
_____	that _____
_____	in the _____
_____	and
and	that choose
_____	
_____	_____
It is for them."	It is for US.

Name_____

Parallel Poetry *(cont.)*

Book Text	Student Poem
"Papagos try _____ _____ . They don't _____ _____ _____ _____ a fox's bones. _____ _____ _____ _____ _____ to people. They never say, '_____ _____ , _____ , '_____ … _____ , *And they do share"*	I try Not to anger _____ . I don't _____ _____ _____ . I don't disturb _____ . I don't shove _____ . I know _____ the same as _____ _____ . I never say, "_____ _____ ." I say, "_____ _____ ." And I do _____ .

Name _____

Date _____

The Papago/Your Family

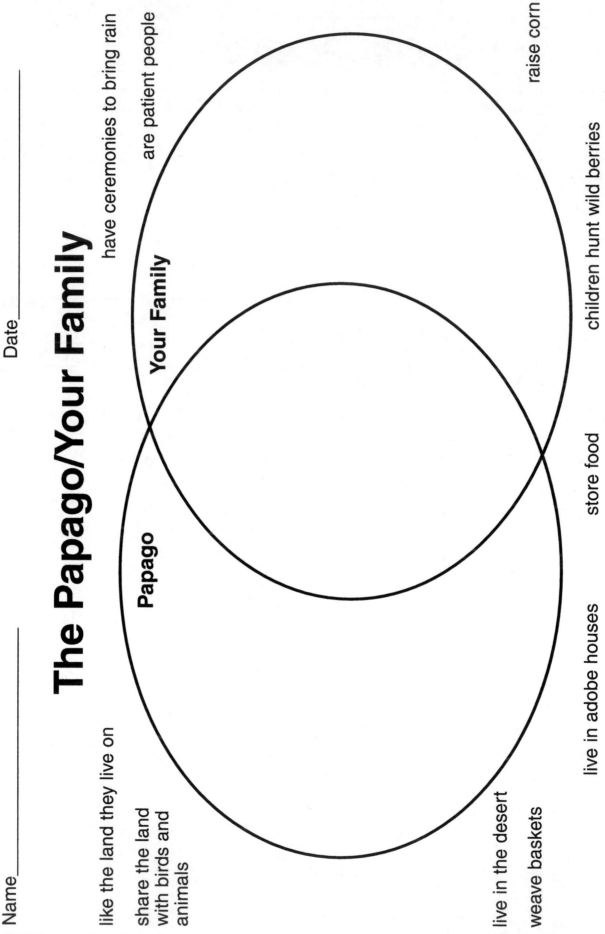

Your Family

Papago

have ceremonies to bring rain

are patient people

raise corn

children hunt wild berries

store food

live in adobe houses

like the land they live on

share the land with birds and animals

live in the desert

weave baskets

Challenge: Make a 3-way Venn diagram for Papago, Navajo, and your family.

The Gift of the Sacred Dog

by Paul Goble

Summary

Factually, we know that horses were brought to North America by the Spanish. However, to the Plains tribes uch a wonderful gift had to be sent to them by the Great Spirit. In The Gift of the Sacred Dog, *Paul Goble tells the Native American version which is rich in language and beautifully illustrated.*

A tribe in search of buffalo was tired and hungry. They had found no buffalo. The people and the dogs were oo tired to go on. A young boy went to the hills to ask the Great Spirit for help. The Great Spirit responded by giving the people the Sacred Dog (the horse) to carry more, to move faster and farther, so the tribe could rind buffalo. Life for the people was good after that. They lived in harmony with all living things and cared For the Great Spirit's gift.

The outline below is a suggested plan for using the various activities that are presented in this unit. You should dapt these ideas to fit your own classroom situation.

Sample Plan

Day I

- Daily Writing Activities (pages 38-40)
- Research the buffalo (use page 26 and other sources)
- Do buffalo math (pages 46-47)
- Make and study Geography of the Plains booklet (page 27)
- Play a Native American game (pages 61-62)
- Homework: Plains Tribes map and word search (pages 28-29)

Day II

- Continue Daily Writing Activities (pages 38-40)
- Research Native Americans and Horses (use page 30 and other sources)
- Create a Picture Story (page 31)
- Read *The Gift of the Sacred Dog*
- Play a Native American game (pages 61-62)

Day III

- Continue Daily Writing Activities (pages 38-40)

- Study and build a tipi (pages 33-34)
- Do Travois Math (pages 44-45)
- Illustrate descriptive language with art project (page 35)
- Play a Native American game (pages 61-62)

Day IV

- Continue Daily Writing Activities (pages 38-40)
- Reread *The Gift of the Sacred Dog* and other legends
- Write an original legend
- Make a musical instrument (pages 55-58)
- Learn a chant and/or dance and accompany with instruments (pages 59-60)
- Play a Native American game (pages 61-62)

Day V *(will take more than one day)*

- Make a Big Book (pages 36-37)
- Do Culminating Activity (pages 64-75)

Overview of Activities

Setting the Stage

1. Use the daily writing activities on pages 38 to 40. Have each child make a small buffalo tag with their name on it to use for answering the daily graph. Do Daily Writing Activity #1 from page 40. Continue daily graphing and writing each day of the unit.

2. Prior knowledge of the role of the buffalo, the horse, and the terrain of the Great Plains will bring a great deal more meaning to *The Gift of the Sacred Dog*. Have the children do the background page on the buffalo (page 26) either as a total class, small group or in pairs depending on the reading level of the group. Make available many other resources on the topic. Students can research and report additional buffalo information.

3. Do the buffalo math (pages 46-47) to add to the students' knowledge about this once plentiful animal.

4. Play a Native American game each day while studying this book (see pages 61-62).

5. Make the Geography of the Plains booklet (page 27). Discuss and research the geographic terms illustrated.

6. For homework, use the Plains Tribes map and Word Search (pages 28 and 29). Have students color the map. Use it for the cover of a folder for the daily writing activities and other work related to this book. It will make an attractive booklet to send home or use for display.

7. Follow the same procedure as in number 2 above for the information page on Native Americans and Horses (page 30).

Enjoying the Book

1. Create a picture story. Directions are on page 31. Display the Picture Dictionary (page 32) for additional symbol ideas. The shortened quote on page 31 is from the beginning of *The Gift of the Sacred Dog,* so this activity will familiarize students with the problem facing the tribe in this story.

2. Show students the cover of *The Gift of the Sacred Dog*. Ask them what the book is about. Why is it titled as it is? Will it be factual or legendary? Then read the note "About the Title" on the back of the title page, the fourth page of this unnumbered book. When students understand that this is a legendary account of the acquisition of horses by the Plains tribes and why this event was worthy of legendary status, read *The Gift of the Sacred Dog* aloud to them. Allow plenty of time for discussion and enjoyment both of the legend and the art work.

Overview of Activities *(cont.)*

3. Have students work with a partner to read About the Tipi and do the experiments on assembling a tipi (page 33). Then make a model tipi (pattern and directions are on page 34). These pages are the basis for the report writing and diorama construction in the culminating research activity on pages 64 to 75, so it is important that the students spend sufficient time. Allow about an hour for pages 33 and 34. Students may wish to do additional research on tipis and the Plains tribes.

4. During math period do the travois math from pages 44 and 45 if appropriate for your students. You can use the introduction and the grid to make up your own math problems for extra credit or homework assignments.

5. Illustrate descriptive language. Use the art project on tissue paper horses (page 35) as a means to have students understand and appreciate the language Goble uses. "There was thunder in its nostrils and lightening in its legs; its eyes shone like stars and the hair on its neck and tail trailed like clouds."

Extending The Book

1. Reread *The Gift of the Sacred Dog.* Share other Native American legends with the children (see Bibliography, page 80 for sources).

2. Have students write their own original legend to explain a phenomenon of nature.

3. Make Native American musical instruments. Many suggestions are on pages 55-58.

4. Learn a chant and/or dance (some suggestions are on pages 59-60) and accompany its performance with the instruments.

5. Make a Big Book. See page 36 for complete directions. Use the skin story technique (page 37) and the tissue paper horse technique (page 35) to create the Big Book. Use the book first as a bulletin board to allow the students to share their work and to reinforce the text and the social studies concepts. After the pages have been displayed for at least a week, then compile the pages into a book and keep in the classroom, share with another class, give to the library, or read to the principal and office staff, etc.

6. Culminate your unit with a Tribal Tribute. Students will do research and prepare reports and visual displays for a Native American tribe of their choice. Refer to pages 64 to 75 for complete directions for this research project.

Name_____

The Buffalo

Buffaloes played an important role in the lives of the Plains tribes. Their meat provided food and their hides were used for clothing and shelter. Bowstrings and sewing equipment were made from buffalo sinew. Bones were crafted into cooking utensils and toys for the children. Rawhide was made into lacings, moccasin soles and parfleches. (Parfleches were skin pouches that were used to carry small utensils and dried meat.)

Hunting for buffalo was no easy task. At first the Native Americans hunted on foot and shot the animals with a bow and arrow. Sometimes hunters would wear a buffalo or wolf skin to mask their human scent so they could get closer to the buffaloes to shoot them. Scouts were sent out to find the herds. Then the hunters lined up in two columns and waved blankets to force the herd toward the edge of a cliff. Other times, buffalo were driven into a corral where they were shot with arrows or clubbed to death.

When Native Americans acquired horses and guns, hunting buffalo became easier. They developed their skills as riders and marksmen. They also became more wasteful and would kill buffalo for sport following in the ways of the white man.

After you have read the paragraph above, write the answers to the clues below. The letters in the boxes will then spell out another name for the American bison.

1. These were made from sinew. ☐ __ __ __ __ __ __ __ __ __ __

2. They were sent to find the herd. __ __ __ ☐ __ __

3. Skin pouches used to carry meat. __ __ __ ☐ __ __ __ __ __ __

4. It was worn to hide human scent. __ __ __ ☐ __ __ __ __

5. These are shot from bows. ☐ __ __ __ __ __

6. They were waved to scare buffaloes. __ ☐ __ __ __ __ __ __

7. Buffaloes were driven here to be shot. __ ☐ __ __ __ __

Answer: ____ ____ ____ ____ ____ ____ ____

26

Geography of the Plains

4 Slopes- a steep slant of a hill or mountain

The horses "were of all colors, galloping down the **slopes**, neighing and kicking their back legs with excitement."

3 Ravine- a small canyon - sometimes called a gorge or chasm

"Looking back he saw the Sacred Dogs pouring out of the cave and coming down the **ravine** toward him."

1 Plain- a large area of flat, treeless land

2 Ridge - the area at the top of a set of hills or mountains

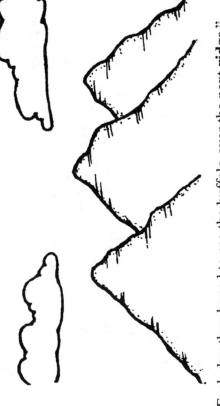

"Each day they hoped to see the buffalo over the next **ridge**."

Tribes of the Plains

Cree

Blood

Blackfoot

Piegan

Assiniboin

Gros Ventre

Crow

Mandan

Santee Sioux

Yankton Sioux

Tenton Sioux

Ponca

Cheyenne

Omaha

Iowa

Pawnee

Arapaho

Osage

Kiowa

Comanche

Apache

The Gift of the Sacred Dog

Tribes Word Search

Use the map on page 28 to help you find the names of 21 Plains tribes.

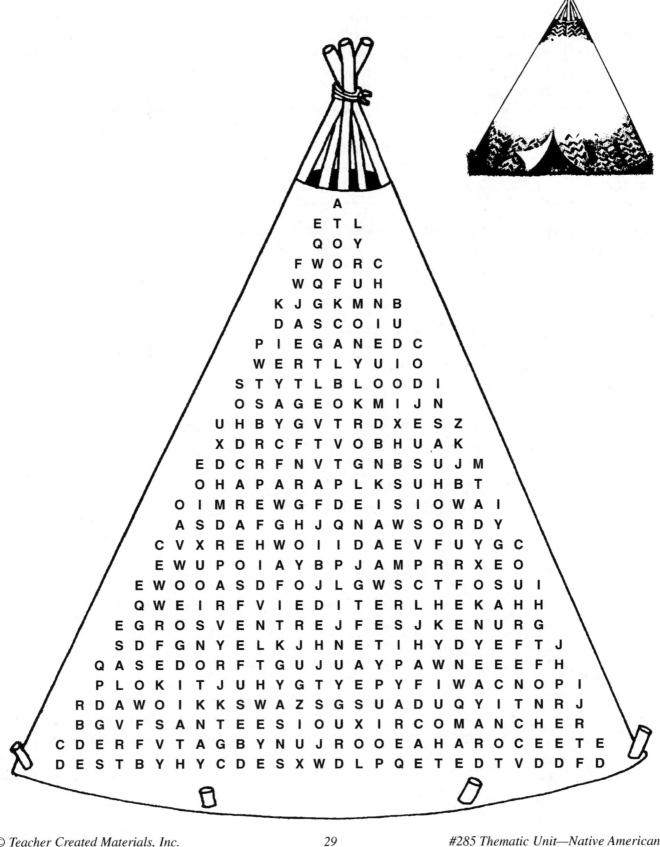

```
                A
              E T L
              Q O Y
            F W O R C
            W Q F U H
          K J G K M N B
          D A S C O I U
        P I E G A N E D C
        W E R T L Y U I O
      S T Y T L B L O O D I
      O S A G E O K M I J N
    U H B Y G V T R D X E S Z
    X D R C F T V O B H U A K
  E D C R F N V T G N B S U J M
  O H A P A R A P L K S U H B T
O I M R E W G F D E I S I O W A I
A S D A F G H J Q N A W S O R D Y
C V X R E H W O I I D A E V F U Y G C
E W U P O I A Y B P J A M P R R X E O
E W O O A S D F O J L G W S C T F O S U I
Q W E I R F V I E D I T E R L H E K A H H
E G R O S V E N T R E J F E S J K E N U R G
S D F G N Y E L K J H N E T I H Y D Y E F T J
Q A S E D O R F T G U J U A Y P A W N E E E F H
P L O K I T J U H Y G T Y E P Y F I W A C N O P I
R D A W O I K K S W A Z S G S U A D U Q Y I T N R J
B G V F S A N T E E S I O U X I R C O M A N C H E R
C D E R F V T A G B Y N U J R O O E A H A R O C E E T E
D E S T B Y H Y C D E S X W D L P Q E T E D T V D D F D
```

Name_____

Native Americans and Horses

Native Americans did not always have horses. It wasn't until the sixteenth century that the Spaniards brought horses to America. At that time, Native Americans still used dogs to carry their packs while hunting. When the Native Americans first saw horses, they called them "big dogs" since they had no word for this new animal in their vocabulary. Southwest Native Americans acquired horses by raiding Spanish settlements. Gradually, they were introduced to the Northern Plains tribes as well. Horses greatly changed the Native American way of life. Now they could travel faster, carry heavier loads, and hunt more easily. War parties rode horses into battle to raid and fight; escape could be made quickly. In time, the horse became a status symbol. The bridegroom's family gave horses to the parents of the bride. Also, wealth was measured by the number of horses owned.

Read the paragraphs above. Then answer the questions.

1. Who brought the first horses to America? _____

   _____

2. What was the Native American name for horses? _____

   _____

3. Where in America were horses first introduced? _____

   _____

4. When was the horse first brought to America? _____

   _____

5. Why were horses important to Native Americans? _____

   _____

6. How did Native Americans first acquire horses? _____

   _____

Challenge:

You are a newspaper reporter. Use your answers to the six questions above to write a news story about the Native American and horses.

A Picture Story

Native Americans of long ago did not have a written alphabet as we do today. Instead, they used symbols to communicate. Sample symbols are on this page and on the Picture Dictionary (page 32). You may create additional symbols as you need them.

Use symbols (no words) to rewrite this quote from *The Gift of the Sacred Dog*.

"The people were hungry. They had walked many days looking for buffalo herds... Even the crows circled, looking for something to eat... wolves called out with hunger at night."

When you have finished, trace this skin pattern and make a neat copy of your picture story on it.

people

hungry

famine (no meat) empty rack outside tipi

three days

many days

buffalo

many buffalo

look

crows

circling

no buffalo

Picture Dictionary

clear weather   rain   snow   no rain   storm

sad   happy   help   war   peace

spring   summer   winter   sun   moon   star

tipi   Indian camp   campfire   good   bad

wise   man   woman   boy   girl   Great Spirit   horse   horse tracks

river   mountains   lake   drum   dancer

bear   eagle   turtle   fish   many fish

Name_____

About the Tipi

The Tipi (tepee) was not just a simple tent. It was a well-constructed home built to stand up to the harsh weather of the Great Plains. It had to be warm in winter to protect from the cold and snow, and cool in the summer to keep people comfortable in the scorching heat. It had to be easily moved from place to place so its people could follow the buffalo herds.

The name tipi comes from two words: "ti" means to dwell, "pi" means used for. The tipi was constructed of a frame of wood poles arranged in a cone shape. This was covered by buffalo hides. The cone shape was very sturdy and could stand up to the very strong prairie winds. Also, there were no pockets to catch water, so it could withstand severe rainstorms as well.

The number of poles for a tipi varied. The average number was about fifteen. These poles were around twenty feet long and weighed fifteen to twenty pounds.

Pitching the Tipi Experiment

Experiment 1: Take fifteen straws and tie them together so they stand up in a cone shape. Describe what happens.

_____

_____

_____

_____

Experiment 2: Now take three (or four) straws and tie them together so they stand up in a cone shape. Describe what happens.

_____

_____

_____

Which way was easier? _____ Why do you think that was? _____

_____

_____

Now you can see why a three (or four) pole frame was used by the Plains tribes. Then the other poles were attached. It was not the men of the tribe, but the women, who were in charge of constructing, transporting and erecting the tipi. The snugness and comfort of the tipi reflected the woman's ability as a housekeeper. A well-made tipi was a source of great pride to a woman.

*Note: This page will also be used with page 69 to practice notetaking.

Name_____

Tipi Pattern

1. Copy pattern on brown construction paper.

2. Draw Native American designs and symbols.

3. Fold along dotted lines.

4. Glue Tab A to Tab B on the inside of tipi.

5. Cut a flap for the door. Add sticks from nature for the poles.

Tab A

Tab B

34

Illustrating Descriptive Language

Materials: a variety of colors of tissue paper (including white, light blue, and black); large sheet of white construction paper per project; starch and small container; paint brush; glitter

Directions For Project I

1. Read the first paragraph from page 16 in *The Gift of the Sacred Dog*

2. Tear black tissue to create the hilltop silhouette. Paint over the area lightly with starch. Put the black tissue on the wet area. Paint over lightly with starch. The starch will work like glue.

3. Tear cloud shapes from white and blue tissue. Put light blue clouds on first using the brush and starch procedure. Add the white clouds leaving an open area in the center of the paper.

4. Cut a large horse from any color of tissue. Put the horse in the center of the paper. Add mane, tail, eye, and hooves from scraps of tissue. Overlapping the tissue intensifies the color and creates a dramatic effect. Add glitter to the mane, tail and eye.

Directions for Project II

1. Read page 19 from *The Gift of the Sacred Dog*.

2. Follow directions 2 and 3 above to create the hilltop and sky.

3. Cut six to eight various colors of tissue paper into 4" x 5" rectangles. Stack them on top of each other. Trace the horse pattern below onto the top piece of tissue. Carefully cut all the pieces together.

4. Separate the horses and add them to the sky in a circular pattern using starch. Add the mane, tails, hooves and details using tissue paper scraps. Add additional clouds so the horses appear to be galloping in them. Add glitter for the stars.

Making a Big Book/Skin Story

The purpose of a Big Book is twofold. First, it is meant to retell the story in a vivid and exciting manner so that students will retain it in their long-term memory. Second, it should provide for extended thinking by challenging the students to read beyond the actual text and recreate it in a different form (synthesis).

Introduce the Project

1. Refer to the picture skin story that the students have already done (page 31.)

2. Demonstrate how to make a skin from a paper bag (page 37).

3. Have the total class give suggestions on completing the first page of the skin story. Then demonstrate how to write the story around in a circle.

4. Lastly, demonstrate how to write a brief narrative to go along with the skin story.

Write the Big Book

1. Divide the class into cooperative groups. These should be groups of three to five that will work well together.

2. Give each group one of the following pages. (The page numbers correspond to pages with text in *The Gift of the Sacred Dog*.)

   page 1—the problem (skin story and narrative)

   page 2—the wise men's attempt to deal with the problem (skin story and narrative)

   page 3—the boy goes to see the Great Spirit (skin story and narrative)

   page 4—he asks the Great Spirit for help (skin story and narrative)

   page 5—the Thunderbirds appear (skin story and narrative)

   page 6—the horse appears (tissue paper horses, page 35)

   page 7—the horses of all colors appear (tissue paper horses, page 35)

   pages 8, 9, and 10—boy comes down from the mountain, horses come from the ravine, boy takes "dogs" to camp (skin story and narrative)

   page 11—to the end of the book—the people greet the horses and commit to caring for them forever (skin story and narrative)

   page 12—Picture Dictionary glossary (Copy page 32 and add the extra symbols used.)

Compile the Book

1. Mount each "skin" on a sheet of butcher paper. Put the narrative at the bottom.

2. Display the big book in mural fashion on the bulletin board so that the children can read each other's words. Later put the pages together as a book and keep in class or donate to the school or public library.

Design Your Own Skin Story

Materials

- Brown grocery bag (¹/₂ bag per student)
- Bucket or sink of water
- Brown and black tempera paint
- Fine tip felt pens
- Scrap paper and pencil for preplanning
- Picture Dictionary (page 32)

Directions

1. Cut out bottom and seam of bag; then cut in half so you have about a square.

2. Crumple the bag; dip it in water; squeeze; remove from water; uncrumple; and repeat twice.

3. Fold the paper in half.

4. Carefully rip out an animal shape as in figure 1 below.

5. Carefully unfold and lay it on a newspaper with any printing up.

6. Mix a little black paint with the brown and paint one side of the "skin" while it is still wet. Cover the printing on the bag.

7. When "skin" is dry, "write" your version of the legend of *The Gift of the Sacred Dog* using your Picture Dictionary. You may need to create some new symbols. If so, add them to your dictionary. Practice on a piece of scrap paper first.

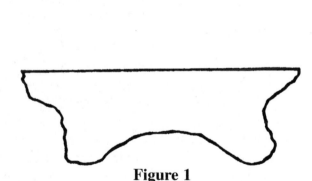

Figure 1

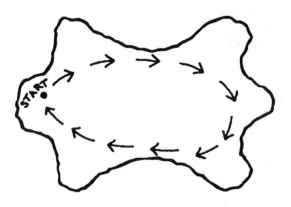

The story should follow a circular pattern as indicated by the arrows.

Extension

Redo the activity and write another (or your own) Native American legend. This can be done as homework.

Attendance Graphing

A Cooperative Learning Activity

This is a unique and relatively easy method of combining a math activity with reading/language arts while having students work both individually and in cooperative groups. It takes from 15 to 30 minutes per day.

First, make a tag for each child in the class. While reading *Annie and the Old One*, use a hogan pattern. While reading *The Gift of the Sacred Dog*, use a buffalo pattern. If you have magnetic chalkboards, attach a magnetic strip to the back of each name tag. These strips can be purchased at a craft store. They can be easily cut with a pair of scissors and have a sticky side so they adhere to the back of the student's tag. If you do not have magnetic boards, you can use double-faced tape.

Second, display one of the graphing questions from page 40 each day either on the chalkboard or another convenient place. As the children enter the room, they use their tag to answer the graphing question before they take their seats—thus, the term "attendance graphing." The absent student's tags will remain in the holding zone. See example:

Holding zone

If you were a Navajo, which job would you prefer?	
Herd sheep?	🛖🛖🛖🛖🛖🛖🛖🛖🛖
Weave rugs?	🛖🛖
Make Jewelry?	🛖🛖🛖🛖

Third, as the students take their seats, they take out their journals. They write down the question and their response. Then they write at least three reasons for their choice. Those that finish early can do an illustration. (While the students do this, you can take roll, collect homework and do other basic chores.)

Group Talk-Around

In groups of three to five, students take turns reading their journal entries. There are three rules for this that should be posted on a chart.

GROUP TALK-AROUND RULES

1. ONLY ONE PERSON SPEAKS AT A TIME.

2. EVERYONE HAS EYE CONTACT WITH THE SPEAKER.

3. EACH PERSON HAS A TURN AND MUST SPEAK LOUDLY ENOUGH FOR EVERY PERSON IN THE GROUP TO HEAR.

Doing this daily gives students practice in writing, listening and speaking. It also gives children a chance to know one another better and fosters a feeling of class unity.

Attendance Graphing *(cont.)*

During Math Period

Students can work in cooperative groups using the round table technique to write summary statements (see below). After the initial training, this should take about 5 to 8 minutes.

First, students should be arranged in groups of four to five. Use the same groups that were used for the Group Talk-Around if possible.

Second, give only one piece of paper and one pencil to each group.

Third, have the students use the attendance graphing information on the board to make true mathematical statements. One child writes his/her statement, then hands the paper and the pencil to the student on the right. The next student writes another statement on the paper and passes the paper and pencil to the right. This continues around the table until the teacher calls time. (Allow about four minutes.) If the group works cooperatively and helps each other out, the paper should be able to go around the group at least three to four times.

Summary Statements

Summary Statements need to be taught for the math activity. Here are some examples of correct and incorrect summary statements using the data from the example on page 38.

THESE STATEMENTS ARE CORRECT

More people in the class would like to be shepherds than weavers.

Fewer people in the class would like to be weavers.

Ten students want to herd sheep.

THESE STATEMENTS ARE NOT CORRECT

Julie wants to be a weaver.

People like to be shepherds.

I would rather make jewelry.

Fourth, once time has been called, have the groups total their responses. The group with the greatest number of responses gets to share their paper with the class. The rest of the class must decide whether the responses are mathematically correct.

Lastly, have the group with the greatest number of correct responses tell the rest of the class how they worked cooperatively to do such a good job.

Daily Writing Topics

These topics can be used for attendance graphing (see page 38) and/or written language activities.

For *Annie and the Old One*

1. If you were a Navajo, which job would you prefer? Tell why.
   Herdsheep   **Weave rugs**   **Make jewelry**

2. Annie took the bus to school. How do you get to school?
   bus   **car**   **bike**   **walk**   **other**

3. Annie was naughty at school. Have you ever been in trouble at school? Tell about what happened in your journal.
   yes   **no**   **sort of**

4. Annie was naughty at home when she let the sheep out of their pen on purpose. Have you ever been bad on purpose at home? If so, tell about it or tell about a friend that you know.
   yes   **no**   **kind of**

5. The Navajos' staple food is ground up maize (corn). Which staple food does your family eat most often? Tell when you eat it and how it is prepared.
   potatoes   **rice**   **bread**   **beans**   **other**

For *The Gift of the Sacred Dog*

1. The Plains tribes used dogs to carry supplies. They fed and cared for these animals. Do you have a pet? How do you feel about it? How do you care for it?
   dog   **cat**   **other**

2. The boy in the story asked the Great Spirit for help for his people. Have you ever tried to help someone in need? Tell about it.
   yes   **no**   **kind of**

3. In the story, wind and hail came with a sudden force. Have you ever been in a storm that scared you? Tell about the experience.
   yes   **no**   **kind of**

4. The people in the story had to look after the horse always. What do you have to look after? Tell what you have to do and how you feel about it.
   Watch little brother/sister   **Take care of my room**
   Take care of pet   **Watch myself until my parents get home from work**

5. Now that you have read about the Plains tribes, would you like to go back in time and be a member of one of the tribes or continue to live in the present? Explain your decision.
   Go back in time   **Live in the present**

Other Non-Graphing Journal Topics *(use at any time during the unit)*

1. Tell how the main character is like you.
2. Tell how the main character is different from you.
3. Write a favorite quote from the book and tell why you selected it.
4. Write a friendly letter to the author. Ask questions, tell what you liked and didn't like about the book.
5. Write a review of the book for a "newspaper."
6. Write a newspaper interview with the main character or a secondary character from the book.
7. Copy a sentence or paragraph that makes you happy and explain why.
8. Complete and explain. The main character reminds me of _____ because _____ .

Comprehension Techniques

The following strategies can be used with many pieces of literature.

Character Web

A character web is a technique which is used to analyze the traits of the main characters in a story. Students must validate their trait selections with specific examples from the literature. This gives a meaningful purpose to rereading which, of course, improves comprehension.

A picture or name of the main character goes in the center circle. The second layer contains the main character's traits. (When teaching this technique, give lots of examples so you don't end up with "pretty" as a trait.) The third layer gives actual examples from the story to support the trait.

By doing a character web for several characters from the same (or more than one) story, students have data to write character comparisons. They can also personalize the literature by completing a web about themselves and comparing it to a book character.

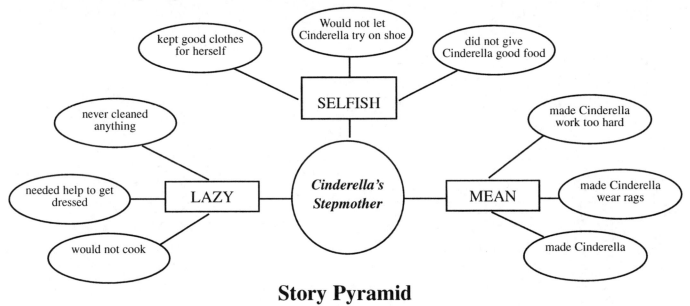

Story Pyramid

This technique is used to look at the main character, story setting, and plot development. At first glance, it appears easy; it is not. Students must be very precise in their word selection. Have students work in pairs or cooperative groups. Have a thesaurus and a dictionary available, as well as copies of the literature selection, if possible.

Line 1 -   One word - main character
Line 2 -   Two words- describe the main character
Line 3 -   Three words - setting
Line 4 -   Four words - state the problem
Line 5 -   Five words - an event
Line 6 -   Six words - an event
Line 7 -   Seven words - an event
Line 8 -   Eight words - solution

Cinderella

Poor Beautiful

Town with Castle

Cannot Attend the Ball

Fairy Godmother Comes to Help

Cinderella Loses One Slipper at Ball

The Prince Puts Glass Slipper on Cinderella

Cinderella Marries Prince and Lives in the Castle

Name_____

Character Web for _____

(name of book)

1. Draw and/or name a character in the center circle.
2. Write three character traits in the surrounding rectangles.
3. Find examples from the book that tell specifically what this character did or said that supports the traits you picked. Write these in the ovals.

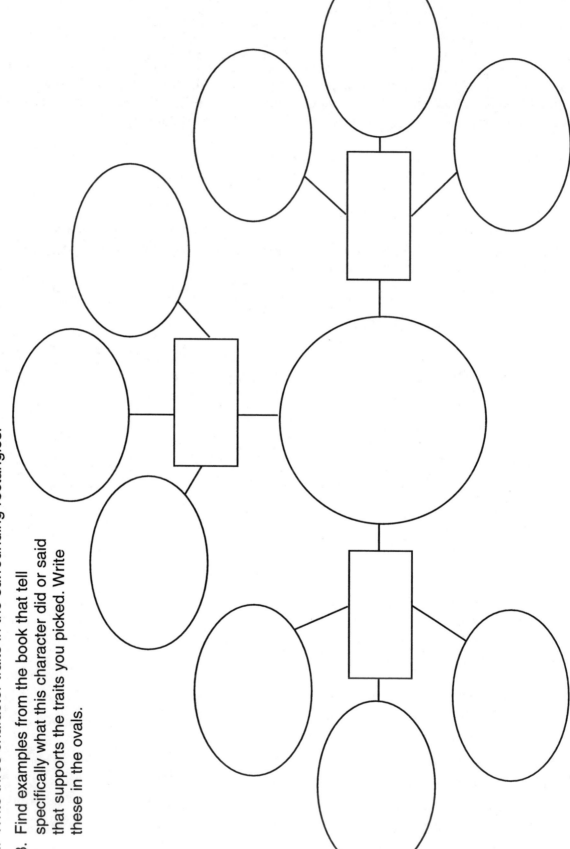

42

Name_____

Story Pyramid

Title of the book: _____

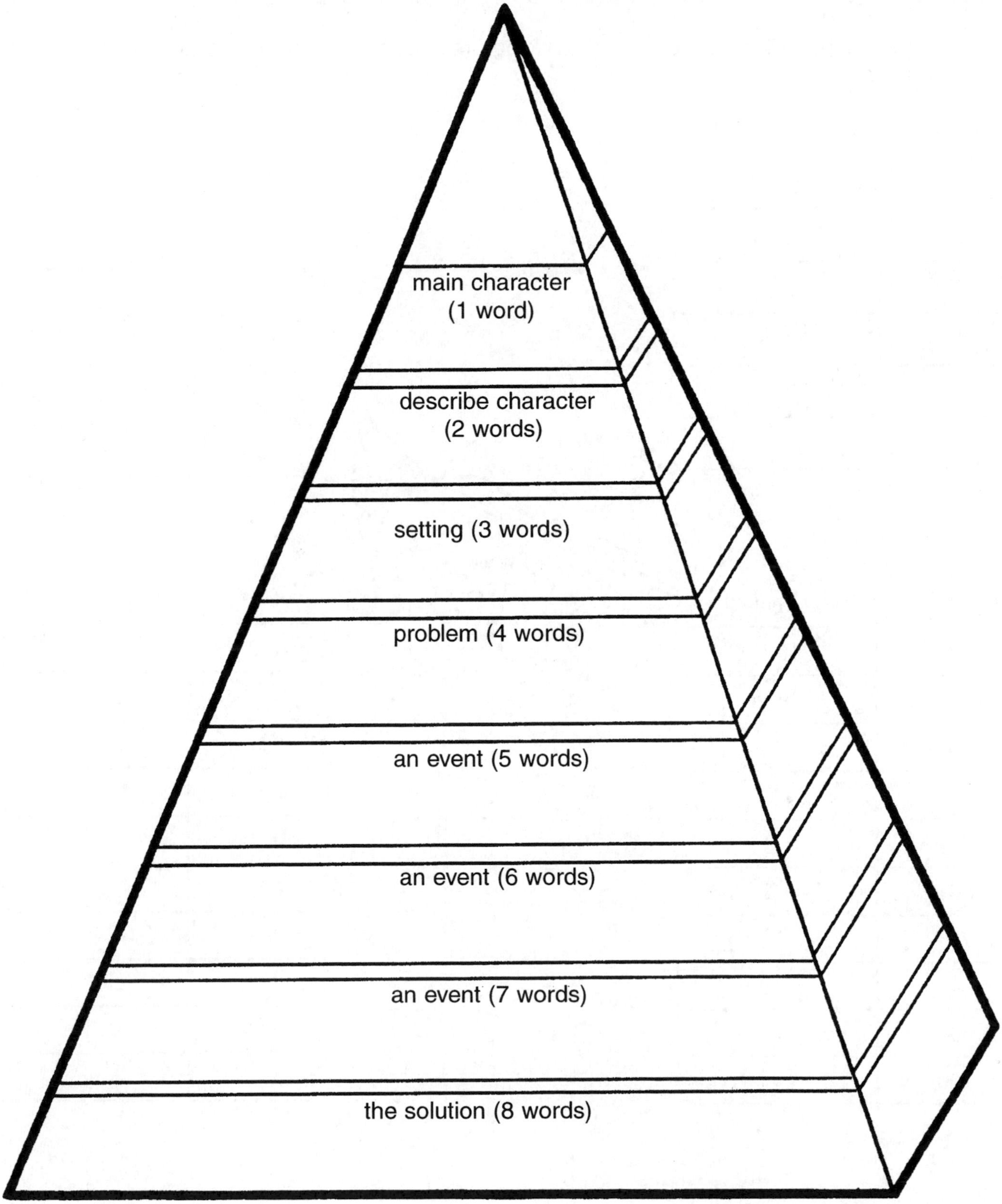

main character
(1 word)

describe character
(2 words)

setting (3 words)

problem (4 words)

an event (5 words)

an event (6 words)

an event (7 words)

the solution (8 words)

Name_____

Travois Math

A travois was a device designed by Native Americans of the Plains to carry supplies as they traveled in search of buffalo. It was pulled first by dog and later by horse.

One dog could pull about 50 pounds (22.5 kilograms). Use this information to fill in the following chart.

# of dogs	weight pulled
1	50 lbs (22.5 kg)
2	
3	
4	
5	
6	

# of dogs	weight pulled
20	
17	
36	
42	
10	
65	

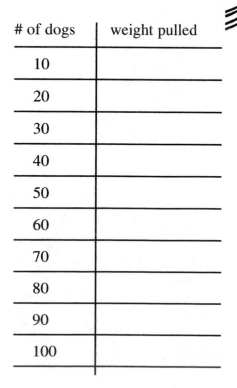

# of dogs	weight pulled
10	
20	
30	
40	
50	
60	
70	
80	
90	
100	

# of dogs	weight pulled
102	
116	
247	
893	
421	
600	
205	
740	
907	
334	

Name_____

Dog Versus Horse

The use of the horse enabled the Plains tribes to travel farther, faster and carry more supplies. Compared to the dog, the horse could go twice as far in a day and could carry four times the weight. Use that information to complete the following tables.

Distance

dog # of km	horse # of km	dog # of km	horse # of km	dog # of km	horse # of km
7			16		20
16			50	16	
25			64		48
37			28		202
63			100	67	
50			42		88
76			90		880

Weight

dog # of km	horse # of km	dog # of km	horse # of km	dog # of km	horse # of km
10			16		20
20			40	16	
30			80		48
40			28		204
50			36	67	
60			8		88
70			32		880
80			12	12	

Name_____

Buffalo Pictograph

Buffaloes are very heavy animals. Bulls, or maies, weigh between 1600 and 2000 pounds (726 to 910 kilograms). Cows, or females, seldom weigh more than 900 pounds (410 kilograms). Read the pictograph below and answer the questions about buffalo weights. Write the answers in word names; e.g., two thousand.

Weight	= 1,000 buffaloes
800 lbs.	🐃🐃🐃🐃🐃🐃🐃🐃🐃
900 lbs	🐃🐃🐃🐃🐃🐃🐃
1600 lbs.	🐃🐃🐃🐃🐃
1800 lbs.	🐃🐃🐃🐃🐃🐃
2000 lbs.	🐃🐃🐃

1. How many buffaloes weigh 1800 lbs? _____

2. How many buffaloes weigh 900 lbs? _____

3. How many buffaloes altogether weigh more than 1600 lbs? _____

4. How many buffaloes altogether weight less than 1600 lbs? _____

5. How many buffaloes are on the pictograph altogether? _____

Challenge:

How many female buffaloes are shown on the graph? _____

How many male buffaloes are shown on the graph? _____

Name_____

Buffalo Facts

How much do you know about buffaloes? You can learn some interesting facts by solving each problem below and writing the answer in the blank. Then read the sentence.

① $42 \div 3 =$ ____ A buffalo has _____ pairs of ribs; humans have only twelve pairs.	**⑤** $15 \times 6 =$ ____ The distance between a buffalo's horns is almost ____ cm (35 in.) at its widest point.
② $560 \div 70 =$ ____ Full-grown bulls (males) stand seven ft. (2.13 m) or ____ ft. (2.43 m) tall at the hump	**⑥** $5 \times 82 =$ ____ Cows (female buffaloes) are much smaller than bulls and seldom weigh more than _____ kg (900 lbs).
③ $130 \times 7 =$ ____ Bulls weigh between 726 kg (1600 lbs) and kg (2000 lbs).	**⑦** $360 \div 60 =$ ____ A buffalo's height at its shoulders is between 5 ½ ft. (1.7 m) and ____ ft. (1.8 m)
④ $700 \div 70 =$ ____ A full-grown bull (male) is ____ ft. (3 m) to 12 ½ ft. (3.8 m) long from the tip of its nose to the end of its tail.	**⑧** $11 \times 50 =$ ____ In 1850, 20 million (20,000,000) buffalo lived on the western plains. By 1899, only _____ were left!

Challenge:

If 19,999,450 buffaloes died in a 50 year period, how many died on the average each year? _____

Find out how and why that many buffaloes died.

Making a Southwest Desert Guidebook

The class will work in small research teams. Each team will develop a field guide for the desert plants and animals mentioned in Byrd Baylor's *The Desert Is Theirs*.

Materials

- 1 copy of page 49 for each student

- 1 copy of pages 50, 51 and 52 for each team

- 10 copies of page 53 for each team (may be duplicated on both sides of paper so that each group will need only 5 papers)

- Crayons, markers or colored pencils

- Encyclopedias and reference books on desert plants and animals

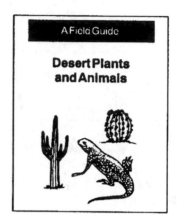

Procedure

1. Complete page 49 as a class to ensure that students understand what to do.

2. Divide the class into teams of five. (There are 20 illustrations provided. This will give four research topics per student.)

3. Have students divide the research topics among their group.

4. Students should research their plants and animals and write their guidebook entry putting the final copy on the guidebook page after the group has helped to edit it.

5. The accompanying picture should be colored, cut out, and glued to the page.

6. The book should be assembled by gluing one copy (chosen by the group) of the scorpion page to the inside of the front cover. The other pages are then inserted, stapled and the book is folded.

7. All class members should be given an opportunity to read and study the completed guidebooks which can be stored near the desert bulletin board.

The Scorpion

Description: _____

Habitat: _____

How it survives: _____

Cut here

Sample Field Guide Page

Read this information about scorpions then fill in the field guide page. Color and cut out the scorpion picture and add it to the page. Use it as a model for additional pages.

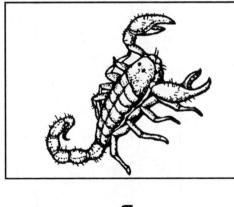

The Scorpion

Scorpions are small desert animals related to spiders. They range from ½ inch to 8 inches (1.3 cm to 20 cm) long. Most scorpions are black or yellowish in color and have six to twelve eyes. Their bodies are made up of two parts. Scorpions have eight legs—the first two are pinchers which are used to catch other small animals. Scorpions live under rocks and stones. They come out at night to hunt for beetles, cockroaches and other small animals. A scorpion stings its prey with a needle that's on the end of its tail. This stuns but does not kill. Only a few scorpions have deadly bites.

A Field Guide

Desert Plants and Animals

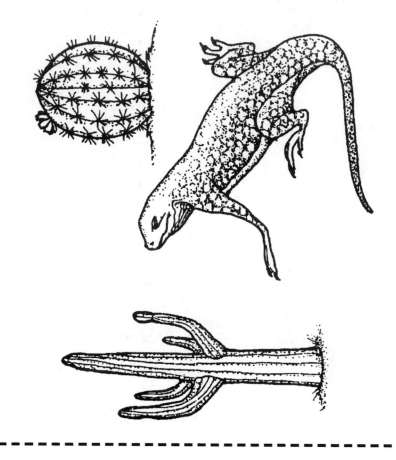

Fold here

Desert Plants and Animals is an identification guide to the plants and animals referred to in *The Desert Is Theirs* by Byrd Baylor. This guide describes and illustrates their physical appearance, their habitat and their method of survival in a harsh environment.

The Authors

This book was written by

Desert Guidebook *(cont.)*
See page 48 for directions.

Coyote

Buzzard

Gopher

Badger

Fox

Deer

Rattlesnake

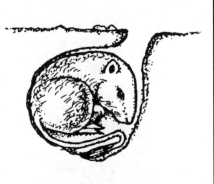

Kangaroo Rat

Pack Rat

Dove

Desert Guidebook *(cont.)*

See page 48 for directions.

Hawk

Toad

Ant

Tarantula Spider

Jack Rabbit

Lizard

Greasewood

Saguaro

Mesquite

Yucca

Fold here

Designing Petroglyphs

Throughout time man has recorded important events in art. Early Native Americans drew or etched their drawings on the walls of caves. These drawings have survived for generations. They are called petroglyphs. Animals and the hunt were often the theme of these cave murals. Drawing an animal's image was a way to possess its spirit and ensure a successful hunt. The artist often signed his work with a handprint.

Materials

for mural: butcher paper as large as you want for your mural (makes a great bulletin board for Parent Night)

for cave: large refrigerator box or voting booths
butcher paper or enough brown grocery bags to cover inside and out

for both: wide, brown crayons   water in containers
watercolor paint (earth tones) and brushes   black or brown poster or tempera paint
twigs or wooden drawing tools to paint with

Directions

1. Discuss the types of petroglyphs created by Native Americans. Some examples are bison, deer, other large mammals, the hunt, village life. Practice drawing some petroglyphs.

2. Prepare the mural or cave surface. Cut butcher paper into manageable sizes. Tape paper to school's outside wall. Have students use the sides of fat, brown crayons to create a rough textured effect on the paper. Once the paper surface is fairly well rubbed by the side of the crayon, remove the mural paper and return to the classroom.

3. In tribal groups, have students select what they are going to create. Practice with the twigs (drawing tools) using tempera paint. When students feel confident, have them paint their petroglyphs on the mural or cave paper. Let dry.

4. After the initial drawing is dry, bring out the watercolors. Stress that Native Americans only had use of colors or dyes that they could make from nature (earth tones): brown, yellow, red, orange, tan.

5. Students then paint their petroglyphs lightly. Let dry.

6. Display petroglyphs as mural or cave drawings.

7. Incorporate oral and written language by having the students write about and discuss their art work.

8. Use the TRIBAL TRIBUNE paper on page 75 to write a news article about the discovery of this amazing and unknown work of ancient art!

Native American Musical Instruments

Music plays an important part in the life of the Native American. From the time he is born until he dies, his life is marked by dancing and ceremony. The drum provides the rhythm and is often joined by rattles and rasps to furnish the background for the chants and dances accompanying tribal ceremonies.

Drums

There are four major types of drums-the small hand drum which could be carried into battle, the larger drum usually made from a hollowed log, the water drum used by the Apache, and the basket drum used by Southwestern tribes.

The drum heads are usually made from hides. The drums are decorated with painted symbols and designs having religious or protective meanings. The Native American never plays the hide drums by tapping with his hands-this is an African method. A drumstick is always used.

Quick and Easy Drums:

1. Coffee cans with plastic lids are instant drum material. First remove metal bottom for better sound. Cover with construction paper. Add Native American symbols and designs.

2. Oatmeal boxes or salt boxes make a different shaped version and can be made in an instant.

3. Paper ice cream containers provide other sizes for these instant drums.

4. Pottery jars, flower pots and metal buckets also make excellent drums. Tie on a head of light 100% cotton canvas. Dampen the fabric to shrink which gives a drumlike sound.

These drums should be struck with beaters. A wooden kitchen spoon with painted Native American designs work well.

5. For a basket drum, use any size woven basket. Turn it over. This can be struck by hand or with pine needles to make a whisk-like sound.

Native American Musical Instruments *(cont.)*

Drums *(cont.)*

Paper and Cloth Drumheads:

Materials:

heavy brown grocery bags	shellac	rubber band
cheesecloth	brush	coffee can for frame (open at both ends)
pencil	wrapping twine	can opener

To Make:

1. Lay cheesecloth over brown paper. (Treat as one piece from now on).

2. Center drum on fabric and trace around it.

3. Cut fabric 2" larger than the circle.

4. Hold fabric/paper under running water to dampen.

5. With cloth uppermost, lay circles on top of can. Hold in place with rubber band.

6. Tie tightly with twine. Leave a loop for holding if desired.

7. Allow to dry thoroughly.

8. Apply 3 coats of shellac allowing head to dry between each coat. (White glue may be used instead of shellac but the sound is not as resonant.)

9. Decorate drum with Native American symbols and designs.

Rattles

Rattles were very important to the Native Americans and they used many different types. Medicine men shook special rattles in ceremonies and healing rituals. Rattles were used as musical instruments during dances and as background to singers. A birchbark rattle accompanied the mournful chant of a Northwest tribal funeral. The Navajo used a combination drumstick rattle made from rawhide soaked around sand and pebbles which could give a drum and rattle sound. Bright paint, feathers, colored ribbon, beads and shells were used to beautify these instruments.

Nineteenth century Native Americans prized the empty metal spice boxes used by the settlers. Tin cans and other metal containers were used for rattles also.

Native American Musical Instruments *(cont.)*

Rattles *(cont.)*

Quick and Easy Rattles:

1. Make a rattle from a cardboard tube. Tape one end of the tube (paper towel, etc.) closed. Place beans inside. Shake to determine sound. Add beans until desired sound is achieved. Tape open end closed. Decorate with marking pens.

2. Use a metal box; a candy or bandage box works well. Put in beans and experiment with sound. Tape box lid closed. Decorate with paper and markers or paint.

Soda Pop Can Rattle:

Materials:

Aluminum soda pop can (clean and dry)

10" dowel, ½ inch diameter

masking tape

beans

construction paper, scissors, marking pens

hammer and nail

Steps:

1. Obtain empty soda pop can. Be sure it's very dry inside (otherwise beans could mold).

2. Insert dowel at the opening. Secure dowel with a nail at the top of can.

3. At bottom opening, insert beans until you have a good sound. The type of bean, rice or popcorn will vary the sound.

4. When you have a sound you like, tape the opening securely.

5. Cover the can with construction paper.

6. Use marking pens and decorate with Native American symbols and/or designs.

Native American Musical Instruments *(cont.)*

Rasps

The rasp (a notched stick) is used by many Native American tribes. By notching sticks in different ways, tribes can vary the sounds and create new sounds to accompany their dances and ceremonies.

The Sioux were able to create an angry bear sound used in the Bear Dance, by rubbing a short heavy rasp with another stick. This was done over a metal sheet covering a hole in the ground. Using this sounding chamber, they created a growl representing the angry spirit of a charging bear.

Quick and Easy Rasp:

Use a piece of corrugated cardboard carton and a pencil or small stick.

More Traditional Rasp (needs to be done in part by an adult):

Materials:

> 1 dowel, 1" diameterby 12"
>
> 1 dowel, ¼" diameter by 8"
>
> saw (coping saw works well)
>
> pocketknife (adult use only!)
>
> pencil
>
> sandpaper

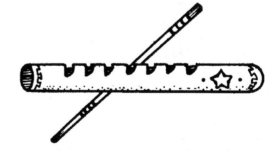

To Make:

1. On the 12" dowel, make a pencil mark every ⅜" from one end, leaving 4" for holding at the other end.
2. With saw, cut straight down into dowel ⅜" at each pencil mark.
3. Have an adult notch a "V" with pocketknife ³⁄₁₆" from each cut.
4. Sand rough edges.

To Play: Rub 8" dowel along the notched dowel.

Ceremonial Chants

Navajo Prayer Chant

The Navajo have a prayer chant, which follows a slow beat of the drum.

May I walk in beauty before me.

May I walk in beauty behind me.

May I walk in beauty below me.

May I walk in beauty above me.

With beauty all around me, may I walk.

Navajo Hogan Chant

This chant was used to bless the newly built hogan, the traditional home of the Navajo people. It was sung and accompanied by drums and rattles. Practice the chant. You may wish to copy it and mark where the drum beats and rattle shakes should go.

There beneath the sunrise stands the hogan.
The house is built of dawn's fair light,

Of fair white corn

Of embroidered robes and hides

Of pure water

Of holy pollen.

There beneath the sunset stands the hogan.
It is built of afterglow

Of yellow corn

Of gems of shining shells.

It is evermore enduring, the hogan blessed.

Papago Rain Ceremony and Chant

This important Papago ceremony takes place once a year in early August. The medicine men pray for rain and good crops. Use the drum, rattle and sticks to accompany this song. Make up your own melody. It is sung with great feeling. It can be used with the rain dance on page 60.

Here I sit

And with my power,

I bring the south wind

toward me,

After the wind

I bring the clouds

After the clouds

I bring the rain

That makes the

flowers grow

That makes the

home ground beautiful.

Creating a Rain Dance

Background

Native Americans held many ceremonies designed to make sure they had the food they needed to survive. These ceremonies almost always included music and rhythmic movement or dance. Singing and chanting was done to the rhythm of handcrafted rattles, drums, rasps, flutes, and/or whistles.

Rain was essential to the farming tribes for their crops and the hunting tribes for the health of the animals they used for food. So, rain dances were often performed in time of drought.

Materials

The whole class

Optional: Rhythm instruments made by class (see pages 55-58)

Directions

mist

1. Students stand in a circle. Everyone must be still and quiet.

2. The leader (either a student or the teacher) begins by rubbing his thumb and two fingers back and forth to make the "mist."

3. He turns toward the person on his right, who then begins rubbing his thumb and two fingers.

4. Each person "passes the mist" until all children are making the mist.

5. The leader then changes his motion to rubbing his palms back and forth. He "passes the drizzle" to the student on his right and so on until all children are making drizzle.

6. The process continuues with "rain"—patting thighs; "downpour"—stomping feet.

7. To end the storm, the process is reversed until the leader is making the mist alone.

drizzle

Extensions

Add rhythms with instruments make by children (directions, pages 55-58).

Add a rain chant created by the class. (See pages 59 for some typical chants.)

Besides improving listening skills, this movement activity encourages concentration and awareness of others.

rain

downpour

Native American Animal Races

Bear Race

This race can be done individually or in teams. The object is to imitate the gait of a bear. The chief who acted as judge rewarded the one who imitated the shuffling run of a bear best, as well as the one who crossed the finish line first. Children line up on the starting line. At the "Go" signal, they put both hands on the ground; then move the right hand and left foot forward at the same time, then the left hand, right foot.

Crab Race

The race was run by Northwestern coastal tribes. All children of this area knew how crabs ran since they saw thousands of them, large and small, along the rocky coast. This race can also be done individually or as a team. Players line up 4 feet apart and sideways to the starting line. At the "Go" signal, they drop to all fours and race, crab fashion, sideways moving right hand, right foot then left hand, left foot to a line about 40 feet away. Then, without stopping or turning around, crawl back to the starting point. Often a "crab" that is fastest to the first line is slower going back when he has to lead with the opposite hand and leg.

Frog Race

This race is run in a fashion similar to the bear and crab races. To imitate a frog, participants clasp fingers around ankles and hop in this squatted position to the finish line. A player who loses his grip is disqualified. A player that falls over can continue as long as he gets back up without releasing his hold on his ankles.

Native American Kicking and Throwing Games

Kickball Races

These races were very popular especially with Southwestern tribes. They varied in length from 1 to 25 miles. The balls ranged from 2 ½ to 4 ½ inches in diameter. They were made of many different materials depending on what was available in the tribe's region. The Pueblo People often stuffed their balls with the hair from fast animals-the horse, the rabbit, and hair from the big toe of a fast runner from the tribe!

The ball for this activity may be a softball or students may make their own. Start with a 1" to 1 ½" diameter rock, add hair from a fast animal if desired, cover with newspaper, and wrap with masking tape. As chief (teacher) you can design this race any way you like. Native Americans ran this race over all types of terrain. They were never allowed to touch the ball with their hands-even if it landed in a river!

Kick Stick Race

This was a popular and strenuous game played by Native Americans. It is played the same way as kickball (above), but uses a stick instead. This stick varied from 2 ½" to 10" long and ¾" to 1 ½" in diameter. A 1" dowel cut about 5" long works very well for our current day usage.

The Zuni believed the stick contained magic that drew the runner along. Each stick was decorated and an owner would never part with a successful stick.

Toss Ball Game

This is a very simple game to do. You will need an old tennis ball that has lost its bounce or a softball. Draw a straight line in the dirt with a stick. Each player in turn must place himself flat on his back, with his shoulders on this line. Place the ball in the palm of the hand. Arm should be outstretched above the head, touching the ground. Player then throws the ball as far as possible. (It doesn't go nearly as far as expected!)

The spot where the ball lands is marked with a stone. The player who throws the ball the farthest is the winner.

Fry Bread

Fry bread is the best known of all the Navajo foods. It is puffy, pastry-like bread. Navajo cooks used handfuls and pinches, but we will use cups and teaspoons.

Ingredients:

2 cups flour

2 teaspoons baking powder

½ teaspoon salt

½ cup powdered milk

warm water

shortening

powdered sugar

Utensils:

frying pan and hot plate or electric frying pan

measuring cups and spoons

tongs

paper towels

large bowl

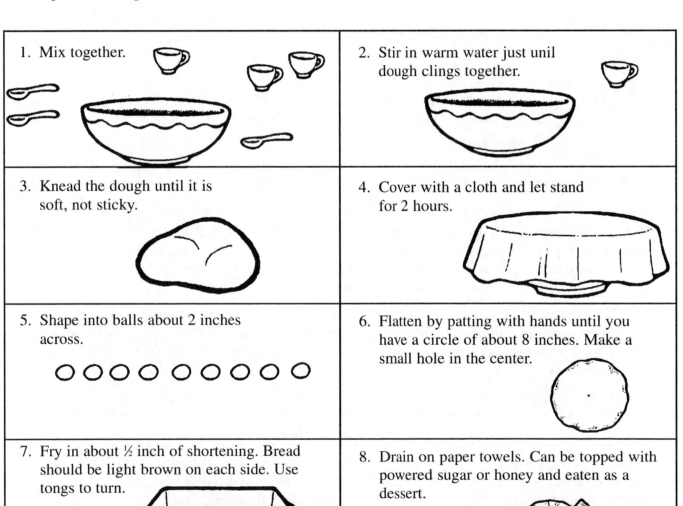

1. Mix together.

2. Stir in warm water just unil dough clings together.

3. Knead the dough until it is soft, not sticky.

4. Cover with a cloth and let stand for 2 hours.

5. Shape into balls about 2 inches across.

6. Flatten by patting with hands until you have a circle of about 8 inches. Make a small hole in the center.

7. Fry in about ½ inch of shortening. Bread should be light brown on each side. Use tongs to turn.

8. Drain on paper towels. Can be topped with powered sugar or honey and eaten as a dessert.

Tribal Tribute:

A Research Center on Native Americans

Teacher Preparation

Make the center. (Directions and patterns are on pages 65-68.) Once the center is completed, save it and you are all set for the next class. Collect reference materials on a variety of Native American tribes. See the Bibliography (page 79) for suggestions. Allow six to ten working periods of 30-60 minutes for completion of all activities. Some of these may be designated as homework.

Introduce the center to the class. Form cooperative groups (teacher or student selection).

Have each group select a tribe for study.

Research Skills

Distribute Practice Note Taking (page 69) and About The Tipi (page 33). Do this as total group lesson, to ensure that students get the idea of writing key words and phrases instead of copying.

Distribute Making Note Cards (page 70). Give out lined 3" x 5" index cards. Have studentslabel their cards by following directions on the page.

Distribute paper on Making A Bibliography (page 71). Again, do this with the total class.

Reports

Allow time for groups to do research on their tribe, write notes on cards, and make bibliographic references. Once research is completed, have groups decide who is responsible for each topic. For example, if Joey is going to write the sections on Clothing and Religion, then all the other members of his group would give Joey their note cards on those topics.

Allow time for students to write and illustrate their sections of the report. After completing their sections, have students read them to their group. The group is responsible for editing. (This needs to be modeled for the average class so no one's feelings get hurt.) Allow time for students to rewrite and add to their group reports.

Distribute Table of Contents (page 72). Have groups fill out and then assemble their reports.

Presentation

Distribute Creating a Visual Display (page 73). Review with the class. Distribute Making An Oral Presentation (page 74). Discuss with the class. Group then needs to decide who is going to be responsible for the visual display and who is going to do the oral presentation. Allow time for the groups to make and practice their sections of the presentation.

Students give oral presentations and explain visual displays to the class. This can be photographed or videotaped. THIS MAKES A GREAT DISPLAY AT PARENT NIGHT OR OPEN HOUSE.

Native American Research Center

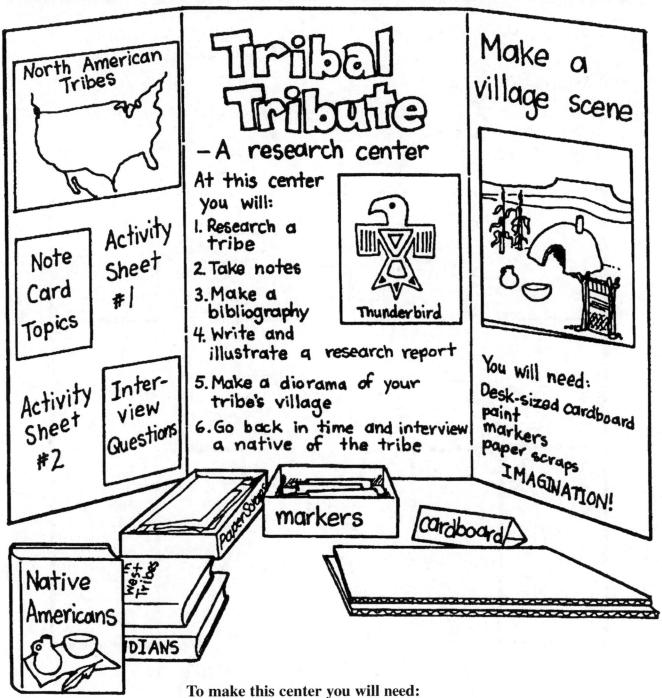

To make this center you will need:

  3 sheets posterboard

  2 manila envelopes

  1 large cardboard sheet per group

  14 3" x 5" lined index cards per group or student

  Lots of paper scraps

  Markers

  Research books on Native Americans

  Duplicated copies of pages 70 and 74

Thunderbird

1. Color and cut out.
2. Attach to research center(see page 65).

This deity was worshipped by almost all North American tribes.

North American Tribes

1. Cut out map pieces (pages 67 and 68).

2. Assemble and glue to construction paper background.

3. Attach to research center (see page 65).

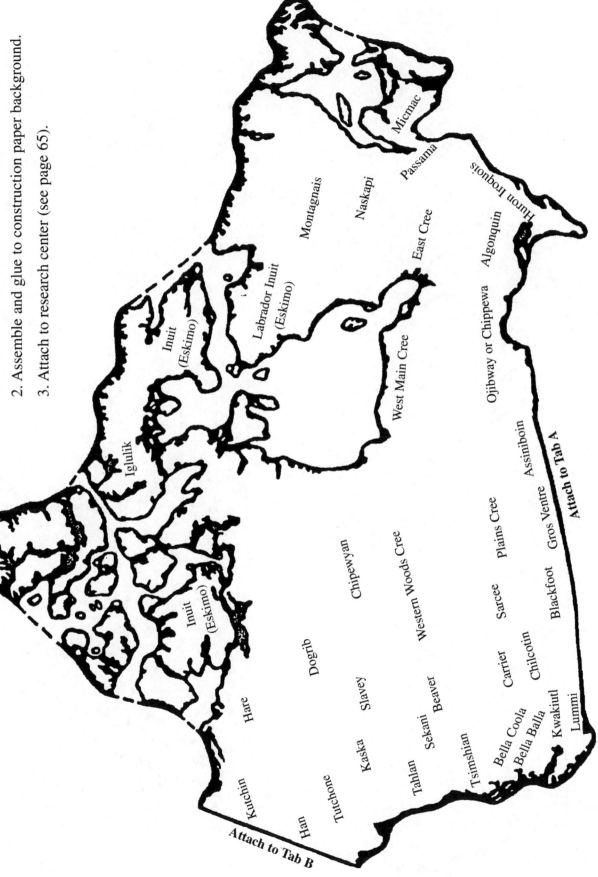

Micmac

Passama

Huron Iroquois

Montagnais

Naskapi

East Cree

Algonquin

Labrador Inuit
(Eskimo)

Inuit
(Eskimo)

West Main Cree

Ojibway or Chippewa

Iglulik

Assiniboin

Gros Ventre

Plains Cree

Attach to Tab A

Chipewyan

Western Woods Cree

Sarcee

Blackfoot

Inuit
(Eskimo)

Dogrib

Slavey

Carrier

Chilcotin

Hare

Beaver

Bella Coola

Kwakiutl

Kaska

Sekani

Bella Balla

Lummi

Tahlan

Tsimshian

Kuchin

Han

Tutchone

Attach to Tab B

North American Tribes *(cont.)*

*See directions on page 67

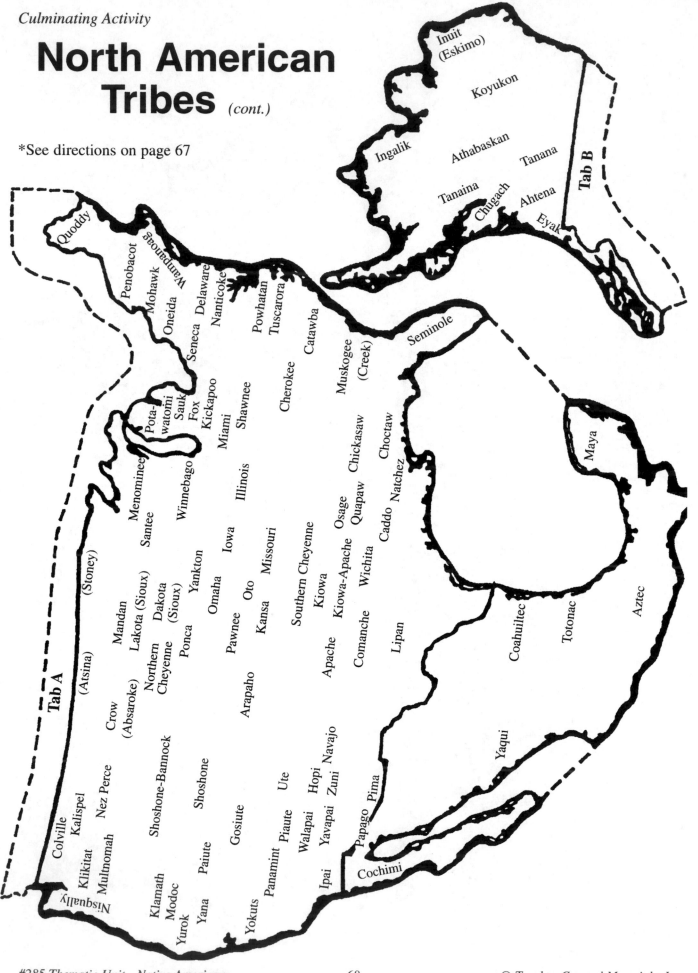

Name_____

Practice Note Taking

When people do research, they do not copy down everything they read about a topic. That would take too long. They take notes. Notes are key words and phrases that help them remember what they have read. After taking notes, researchers write out the information in sentence form.

Before you begin your official research on your selected tribe, practice taking notes. Read about tipis (page 33). On the lines below write down 10 key words or phrases. Then compare them to the ones used when the article was written (see below). Yours shouldn't be the same, but they should appear similar. Most importantly, they should help you remember what you read.

1. _____

2. _____

3. _____

4. _____

5. _____

6. _____

7. _____

8. _____

9. _____

10. _____

- -

easy to move   cool for summer   warm for winter   well-constructed

15 poles   buffalo hides   frame of 3 or 4 poles   women responsible

waterproof   cone was windproof

Name_____

Making Note Cards

For your report on Native Americans, you will need to take notes. On each of your 3x5 index cards, cut and paste one of the following headings.

TRIBAL NAME	HABITAT
TRIBAL NAME	FOOD
TRIBAL NAME	CLOTHING
TRIBAL NAME	SHELTER
TRIBAL NAME	TRANSPORTATION
TRIBAL NAME	GOVERNMENT
TRIBAL NAME	RECREATION
TRIBAL NAME	ART AND MUSIC
TRIBAL NAME	LANGUAGE/ COMMUNICATION
TRIBAL NAME	RELIGION
TRIBAL NAME	ROLE OF MAN AND WOMAN
TRIBAL NAME	RAISING CHILDREN
TRIBAL NAME	OTHER INTERESTING FACTS
TRIBAL NAME	OTHER INTERESTING FACTS

TAKING NOTES:

As you read interesting information, write key works or phrases on the note cards. Remember that someone else may have to read and understand them so be neat and careful.

Tribal Name <u>Navajo</u>	Role of Man and Woman
Women –	Weave
	sell rugs
	in charge of hogan
Men –	jewelry making
	turquoise
	herding sheep

Name_____

Making a Bibliography

A bibliography is very important to a research report. It tells the reader where you got your information. If there is ever any question about a fact, you can find the source in the bibliography.

There is an exact way to write a bibliographic entry. Certain information must be included. Every time you read a book about your subject, make a bibliographic note card like this:

Bibliography

Author: (Last name, First name)

Title: (Name of the book)

Publisher: (Name of publishing company)

City, State: (Where the book was published)

Year: (When the book was published)

This information can usually be found on the title page and the following page of a book. Look at these examples:

Find the following on the pages above. Mark and color code them.

1. Author (red)	2. Title (blue)	3. Publisher (green)
4. City (yellow)	5. State (orange)	6. Year (purple)

A correct bibliographic entry for the book above would be:

Youngbird, Sue. **All About the Tipi.** Coan Books, Inc., Chicago, Illinois, 1987.

Table of Contents

_____

(TRIBE)

WRITTEN BY

_____

_____

_____

_____

DATE: _____

Creating a Visual Display

Diorama of a Tribal Scene

With your group, you will create a village scene depicting the life of your tribe.

Materials

1 desk-sized cardboard,

paper scraps, markers,

crayons, dirt, sand, leaves,

twigs

IMAGINATION

COOPERATION

INFORMATION

Procedure

1. Using the desk-sized cardboard, make the environment of your tribe. Did they live in the forest, the desert, near the ocean? Use dirt, sand, leaves and twigs to create the land for the tribe.

2. Create the tribal homes. Did they live in large groups, small groups, single dwellings? Did they live in a tipi, hogan, longhouse?

3. Make men, women and children of the tribe. Add them to your diorama. How did they dress? What activities did they do? Have them doing those activities.

4. Did your tribe farm? Hunt? Herd animals? Be sure your display shows this.

5. What type of cooking utensils did your tribe use? Did they make baskets? Did they make pottery? Have them in your display.

6. What type of weapons did your tribe use? Add them to your diorama.

7. Think of what else would have been included in a village scene. The more your group can include, the better others can understand the customs, culture and life of your tribe.

Name_____

Making an Oral Presentation

An Interview with a Native American

You are a reporter for the *Tribal Tribune*. You are able to go back in time with the aid of your imagination and a time machine. You interview a person of your own age that is a member of the tribe you have been studying. You want to find out as much as possible about this person so that the readers of the *Tribal Tribune* can have the same experience that you have had. You believe it is important that people generations and cultures apart can know and understand each other. Ask these questions and any others that you or your group think are significant. Report them in the newspaper, the *Tribal Tribune*. Then practice a live TV interview with your Native American. You can use the same questions, but practice them so they seem natural and not read from a script.

QUESTIONS:

What is your name?
Why are you called that?
Tell me about your family.
What kind of chores do you do?
What do you do for fun?
Describe your home.
What is the weather like where you live?
What do you and your family eat?
What type of clothing do you wear?
How do you get your food?
What jobs does your father have?
What jobs does your mother have?
What is the best thing about being a member of your tribe?
What is special about your tribe?
If you could say something to children of the future, what would that be?

OTHER QUESTIONS:

_____

_____

_____

_____

_____

_____

Write the answers to the questions on a separate sheet of paper as your rough draft. Then redo them as a newspaper interview for the *Tribal Tribune*. Use the *Tribal Tribune* paper (page 75) for your final copy.

Tribal Tribune

Volume I   **Date:**

Meet A Native American

by _____

_____

_____

_____

_____

_____

_____

_____

_____

_____

_____

_____

_____

_____

_____

_____

_____

_____

See column 2

Native Amencan, _____ , *at his home in*

name

a _____*village.*

tribe

column 2

_____

_____

_____

_____

_____

_____

_____

_____

_____

_____

_____

_____

_____

_____

Bulletin Board

Objectives

This interactive bulletin board can be used to identify land forms, animals and plants of the desert. New concepts are added to the background as they are studied.

Materials

blue butcher paper	pushpins or straight pins	sandpaper, burlap, tissue or crepe paper
scissors	stapler	construction paper

Construction

- Staple a blue background to the bulletin board to make the sky.
- Staple sandpaper, burlap, tissue or crepe paper to the bottom of the background to create the desert.
- Duplicate the land form patterns on pages 77 and 78. Color, cut out and add to the background. Label them.
- Enlarge the plant and animal patterns (pages 51 and 52) on an overhead projector. Or have students draw them.
- Make a sun from yellow construction paper or tissue.

Directions

- Add the plant and animal patterns to the bulletin board background as they are studied. Assign different ones to small groups. Label the plants and animals once they have been attached to the board.
- Evaluation Activity: Remove all labels. Have the students identify the various plants, animals and land forms.
- Evaluation Activity: Play Twenty Questions where one student chooses a land form, plant or animal and the other students ask questions to determine what he is thinking of.

Bulletin Board Pattern

Fold a sheet of construction paper or tissue in half. Place dotted line of pattern on the fold. Cut out.

Mesa

Place on fold of paper

Bulletin Board Pattern

Fold a sheet of construction paper or tissue
in half. Place the dotted line of pattern on
the fold. Cut out.

Butte

Place on fold of paper

Bibliography

The number of excellent books on this topic is almost infinite. The following bibliography lists a few that are written at a student's reading level.

Background Information

Erdoes, Richard. *The Native Americans: Navejos.* Sterling Publishing Co., Inc., New York, 1978.

Freedman, Russell. *Buffalo Hunt.* Holiday House, New York, 1988.

Gates, Frieda. *North American Indian Crafts.* Harvey House Publishers, New York, 1981.

Glass, Paul. *Songs and Stories of the North American Indians*. Grosset & Dunlap, New York, 1970.

Gridley, Marion E. *The Story of the Navejo*. G.P. Putnam's Sons, New York, 1971.

Hofsinde, Robert (Gray-Wolf). *Indian Arts.* William Morrow and Company, New York, 1971.

Sheppard, Sally. *Indians of the Plains.* Franklin Watts, New York, 1976.

Yue, David and Charlotte. *The Tipi: A Center of Native American Life*. Alfred A. Knopf, New York, 1984.

Native American Legends

Bierhorst, John. *Doctor Coyote: A Native American Aesop's Fables.* MacMillan, New York, 1987.

Caduto, Michael J. & Joseph Bruchac. *Keepers of the Earth: Native American Stories and Environmental Activities for Children.* Fulcrum, Inc., Golden, Colorado, 1988.

dePaola, Tomie. *The Legend of Bluebonnet.* G.P. Putnam's Sons, New York, 1983.

Goble, Paul. *Buffalo Woman*. Bradbury Press, Scarsdale, New York, 1984.

Goble, Paul. *The Girl Who Loved Wild Horses*. Bradbury Press, New York, 1978.

Goble, Paul & Dorothy Goble. *Lone Bull's Horse Raid.* Bradbury Press, New York, 1973.

Goble, Paul. *Star Boy.* Bradbury Press, New York, 1983.

McDermott, Gerald. *Arrow To The Sun: A Pueblo Indian Tale.* Puffin Books, New York,1977.

Morgan, William. *Navajo Coyote Tales.* Ancient City Press, Santa Fe, New Mexico, 1988.

Poetry

Allen, Terry. *The Whispering Wind: Poetry by Young American Indians.* Doubleday, New York, 1972.

Baylor, Byrd. *Hawk, I'm Your Brother.* Charles Scribner's Sons, New York, 1976.

Baylor, Byrd. *The Other Way to Listen*. Charles Scribner's Sons, New York, 1972.

Baylor, Byrd. *When Clay Sings*. Charles Scribner's Sons, New York, 1972.

Jones, Hettie. *The Trees Stand Shining.* Dial Press, New York, 1971.

Sneve, Virginia Driving Hawk. *Dancing Teepees: Poems of American Indian Youth.* Holiday, New York, 1989.

Answer Key

p. 26

1. bowstrings
2. scouts
3. parfleches
4. wolf skin
5. arrows
6. blankets
7. corral

Down: buffalo

p. 29

Wordsearch

p. 30

1. The Spaniards
2. big dogs
3. Southwest
4. 16th century
5. Horses allowed Native Americans to travel faster, carry heavier loads and hunt more easily.
6. by raiding Spanish settlements

p.44

1. 50 lbs-22.5 kg
   100 lbs-45 kg
   150 lbs-67.5 kg
   200 lbs-90 kg
   250 lbs-112.5 kg
   300 lbs-135 kg

p. 44 (cont.)

2. 1,050 lbs-472.5 kg
   850 lbs-382.5 kg
   1,800 lbs-810 kg
   2,100 lbs-945 kg
   600 lbs-270 kg
   3,250 lbs-1,462.5 kg

3. 500 lbs-225 kg
   1,000 lbs-450 kg
   1,500 lbs-675 kg
   2,000 lbs-900 kg
   2,500 lbs-1,125 kg
   3,000 lbs-1,350 kg
   3,500 lbs-1,575 kg
   4,000 lbs-1,800 kg
   4,500 lbs-2,025 kg
   5,000 lbs-2,250 kg

4. 5,100 lbs-2,295 kg
   5,800 lbs-2,610 kg
   12,350 lbs-5,557.5 kg
   44,650 lbs-20,092.5 kg
   21,050 lbs-9,472.5 kg
   30,000 lbs-13,500 kg
   10,250 lbs-4,612.5 kg
   37,000 lbs-16,650 kg
   45,350 lbs-20,407.5 kg
   16,700 lbs-7,515 kg

p. 45

1.		2.	
14 km		8 km	
32 km		25 km	
50 km		32 km	
74 km		14 km	
126 km		50 km	
100 km		21 km	
152 km		45 km	

p. 45 (cont.)

3.		4.	
10 km		40 kg	
32 km		80 kg	
24 km		120 kg	
101 km		160 kg	
134 km		200 kg	
44 km		240 kg	
440 km		280 kg	
		320 kg	

5.		6.	
4 kg		5 kg	
10 kg		64 kg	
20 kg		12 kg	
7 kg		51 kg	
9 kg		268 kg	
2 kg		22 kg	
8 kg		220 kg	
3 kg		48 kg	

p. 46

1. 6,000
2. 7,000
3. 9,000
4. 16,000
5. 30,000

Challenge:

16,000 female

14,000 male

p. 47

1. 14
2. 8
3. 910
4. 10
5. 90
6. 410
7. 6
8. 550

Challenge:

399, 989